LITTLE QUICK FIX:

KNOW YOUR VARIABLES

#LittleQuickFix

Sara Miller McCune founded SAGE Publishing in 1965 to support the dissemination of usable knowledge and educate a global community. SAGE publishes more than 1000 journals and over 800 new books each year, spanning a wide range of subject areas. Our growing selection of library products includes archives, data, case studies and video. SAGE remains majority owned by our founder and after her lifetime will become owned by a charitable trust that secures the company's continued independence.

Los Angeles | London | New Delhi | Singapore | Washington DC | Melbourne

KNOW YOUR VARIABLES

John
MacInnes

Los Angeles | London | New Delhi
Singapore | Washington DC | Melbourne

Los Angeles | London | New Delhi
Singapore | Washington DC | Melbourne

SAGE Publications Ltd
1 Oliver's Yard
55 City Road
London EC1Y 1SP

SAGE Publications Inc.
2455 Teller Road
Thousand Oaks, California 91320

SAGE Publications India Pvt Ltd
B 1/I 1 Mohan Cooperative Industrial Area
Mathura Road
New Delhi 110 044

SAGE Publications Asia-Pacific Pte Ltd
3 Church Street
#10-04 Samsung Hub
Singapore 049483

First published 2019

Editor: Mila Steele
Production editor: Ian Antcliff
Marketing manager: Ben Griffin-Sherwood
Design: Shaun Mercier
Typeset by: C&M Digitals (P) Ltd, Chennai, India
Printed in the UK

Library of Congress Control Number: 2018958984

British Library Cataloguing in Publication data

A catalogue record for this book is available from the British Library

ISBN 978-1-5264-5884-1

At SAGE we take sustainability seriously. Most of our products are printed in the UK using responsibly sourced papers and boards. When we print overseas we ensure sustainable papers are used as measured by the PREPS grading system. We undertake an annual audit to monitor our sustainability.

Contents

Everything in this book!

Section 1 Variables are important. Societies, and the people who make them up, are in constant motion. In order to be able to describe and measure them we have to think in terms of variables.

Section 2 Variables describe a feature of a person, organization or society. We cannot 'see' them directly, so we measure cases to find the value that each one takes for the variable we are interested in.

Section 3 The more clearly and carefully a variable is defined, the better. The language of variables, values and cases may not always be used explicitly, but to help spot the variable we can **ask questions like who, when and where?**

Section 4 Since the characteristics that describe a person or organization vary in different ways we have **two main kinds of variable.** Continuous variables measure characteristics that vary quantitatively, like age. Categorical variables classify cases into different groups or categories, like sex.

Section 5 Examining relationships between variables is the basic building block of all social science. We can **examine categorical variables through tables and continuous variables through scatterplots.**

Section 6 Often we are interested in **how one variable varies with one or more other variables.** Even if we have no direct evidence of cause and effect it can be useful to think of one variable as dependent on one or more independent variables.

Section 7 **Just because two variables are correlated does not mean one causes the other.** While a relationship, correlation or association between two variables is necessary for there to be a relation of cause and effect between them, this is not sufficient evidence.

Section 8 **How you use variables will depend on the kind of project you undertake.** Qualitative research can use a large number of variables but only a few cases in depth, while quantitative research can use a larger number of cases but with more tightly defined variables.

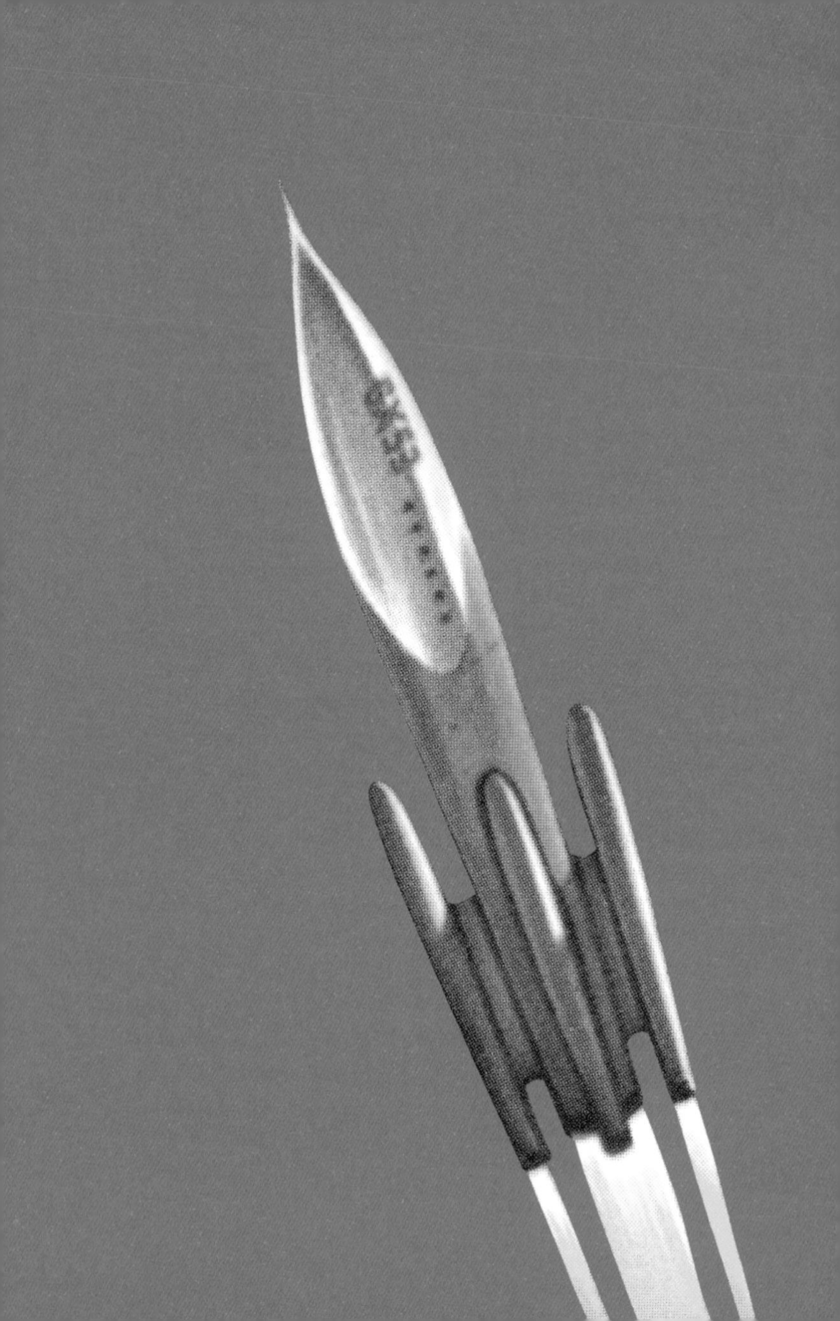

Section 1

Variables are important

Why do variables matter?

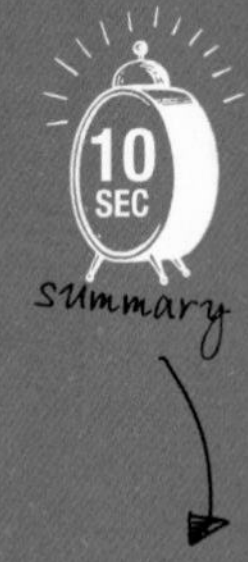

To describe anything, we need to measure it.

Variables are vital

Variables are what we use to measure the beliefs and behaviour of individuals and the institutions, organizations and societies they live in. These characteristics, behaviour and beliefs are enormously variable and constantly changing.

In the natural world, the behaviour of inanimate objects can be described by laws that we do not expect to change. The boiling point of water, force of gravity or speed of light does not change from one week to the next. The social world could hardly be more different. While there may be some constants in human belief and behaviour, it is the phenomenal variation that is most apparent. We meet the challenge of describing, making sense of and finding patterns in this variation by using variables and examining the relationships between them.

WHY WE NEED VARIABLES

Measurement is the basis of all science, social or natural, because if something exists it can be measured, even if you cannot see it.

We can measure how unhappy or content someone is, their ethnicity, views about politics, their kin or friendship networks, educational qualifications, occupation, income or any other characteristics we might discover by consulting records or interviewing them.

MEASURING CHARACTERISTICS AND MAKING COMPARISONS

Usually we are less interested in individuals than in social groups and making comparisons between them. We might want to examine distribution of income or other resources in a society, compare political behaviour of different age groups, examine educational qualifications of different genders, and so on.

Our interest might also be in organizations, institutions, governments or entire countries. Just like individuals, we can measure their characteristics and make comparisons. We might look at average life expectancy and wealth across countries, or compare fertility, literacy or suicide rates for their populations.

WHY VARIABLES ARE IMPORTANT IN THE SOCIAL SCIENCES

In the social sciences measurement is especially important because variation is everywhere and societies are in constant motion.

One carbon atom is pretty much like any other, and the way it might behave in the future is limited by the laws of chemistry and physics. Not so for people. Each individual is unique, and their range of belief and behaviour astonishing. This rarely conforms strictly to any 'law' of the kind natural scientists can use to describe things.

WHY VARIATION IS CHALLENGING TO MEASURE

Variation occurs over both time and space. People are mobile, geographically and socially. Across their lives they will mature from largely helpless infants to adults with a wide, complex range of social roles and obligations.

Institutions, organizations and entire societies evolve and change over time, too. Even the most successful corporations might only last a few decades. Look at a world map from a century ago: not only have the names of countries changed, but also the borders between them.

Thus any collection of examples from the 'same' group will still exhibit a tremendous variety of characteristics.

People believe in different religions or none. Companies have large or small turnovers, make grand profits or dreadful losses, grow or decline. Tests on subjects of a psychological experiment will reveal divergent results.

HOW TO GET YOUR HEAD AROUND VARIATION

Because we need to make sense of all this variation, the basis of all social measurement, and all data, is variables. Variables allow us to make comparisons between different societies, groups of people, or individuals.

Variables do this by each describing a single feature of a person, organization or society that changes over time or across different examples of the same thing. Anything that can describe a feature of a person, organization or a society can be treated as a variable.

We can build up comprehensive descriptions of societies and social relations by measuring several variables. We can measure as many variables as we need to build up an adequate description of whatever we want to know.

USING VARIABLES TO ANSWER QUESTIONS

These variables then allow us to make comparisons, and establish correlations, which are the building blocks of social science. They allow us to answer questions like

Is gender inequality greater in Western or Eastern Europe?

Is social mobility declining?

Are young women more or less 'feminist' than their mothers?

Has violence declined over the last century?

Are people who can read and write more liberal in their attitudes?

Are richer societies also happier ones?

Got it?

Q: Why do we need variables to describe societies, organizations and the people who make them up?

Got it!

A: Because societies, organizations and people are heterogeneous and change so much over time. We need variables to describe their features and explore the relationships between them.

Variables describe a feature of a person, organization or society

Section

What is a variable?

A variable is a way to capture variation and measure the values it takes across cases.

Defining the variable as a question

Many interesting variables, like class, race, gender or inequality, are not directly visible. However, we can still measure them by defining how they affect the characteristics, behaviour or thoughts of people, organizations or societies.

Variables take the form of measuring these features – finding their values – across many cases to see how they vary. It is often useful to think of a variable as a question, and the values it can take as all the possible answers to that question. To get clear answers, the question, and the variable, need to be carefully defined.

MEASURING THE INVISIBLE

Have you ever seen a variable?

You cannot see height, weight, income, ethnicity, happiness, gender, gross domestic product, religion or almost any important, interesting social characteristic. But we can see, and measure, a person by height or weight, check their income records, or ask about their religious beliefs. Governments can use tax returns and surveys to estimate the size of the economy or gross domestic product.

So, to see and measure a variable we examine cases.

A case is always either an individual person or some kind of social unit, like a family, household, company, firm, institution, club or even an entire country or state.

To build up a description of a case we think of the various variables we could use to describe it, and how they might be measured.

We then measure the value a variable takes for each case we examine.

DO IT YOURSELF

HOW TO DEFINE CASES IN TERMS OF VARIABLES

Think of how you might describe yourself as a case in terms of variables. Simple ones to start with might be your age or sex, or whether you are a student. Try to write down ten of them.

1 ....

2 ....

3 ....

4 ....

5 ....

6 ....

7 ....

8 ....

9 ....

10 ....

Then think of the university or college you are studying in (*not* the individual people in it) as a case and write down five possible variables. Two variables could be the number of students studying there and its location.

1 ....

2 ....

3 ....

4 ....

5 ....

Turn the page for some possible answers!

POSSIBLE ANSWERS

DO IT YOURSELF

Person

name; sex; age; ethnicity; religion; place of birth; nationality; hair colour; hairstyle; eye colour; height; weight; anxious/laid back; talkative/quiet; tidy/messy; radical/conservative; always comes to class/rarely comes; gay/straight; weekend job/no weekend job; year at university; stays in flat/student residence/at home; drinks rarely/often; smoker/non-smoker; sporty/couch potato; favourite music, film, book, play; owns a bike or not

University/college

name; location; when established; number of students; number of staff; number of degrees it offers; number of campuses; proportion of mature students

SEEING VARIABLES AS QUESTIONS AND ANSWERS

If you look at your answers you will see that when you consider a variable, you also have to think about how to measure it. A useful way of approaching this is to think of a variable as a question, and then consider the different answers that would describe different cases. Such as

Sex?............................**Man, Woman, Transgender**

Age?............................**Number of years since birth**

Whether voted at
last election?..................**Yes, No, Don't remember**

Marital status?...............**Single, cohabiting, civil partnership, married, separated, divorced**

TURNING THESE QUESTIONS INTO MEASURABLE VALUES

When we define a variable, we call the answers to these questions the values the variable can take. We can then observe the value each case takes for a variable.

If we wanted to examine the strength of religious feeling in a society, our cases could be a sample of individuals from that society. We could collect information about whether they thought of themselves as belonging to a religion. This would be our variable. The values of the variable could be 'Belong; Do not belong; Don't know; No answer'.

We might compare the unemployment rate in different countries. The cases would be the countries we collected data on. The variable would be unemployment. The values would be rate of unemployment in each of the countries.

IDENTIFYING VARIABLES, VALUES AND CASES

Identify the variables, values and cases in the following statements. Check your answers against the correct answers in the chart on the following page.

1 In a recent study of workers in the UK, it was found that 6.2 million were members of a trade union.

2 In a 2016 survey, 67% of adults in Europe said that 'gays and lesbians should be free to live life as they wished', while 22% disagreed.

3 According to the US Census Bureau, in 2017, 61% of Americans identified as White, 18% as Hispanic, 12% as Black and 6% as Asian.

4 In Western Europe the average height of adult males grew from 166cm at the start of the nineteenth century to 178cm in 1980.

5 Gross domestic product per person (a measure of the wealth of a country) was estimated to range from $700 in the Central African Republic to $128,378 in Qatar.

ANSWERS

	Variables	Values	Cases
1	Union membership	member; not a member.	workers in the UK
2	Views on gay rights	agree; disagree	adults in Europe in 2016
3	Race identity	White; Hispanic; Black; Asian	residents of the USA in 2017
4	Height	cm	adult males in Western Europe 1800–1980
5	GDP	USD ($)	countries of the world

I can measure variables by examining the values they take for different cases or observations.

Section

Ask questions like who, when and where?

How do I identify a variable?

The language of variables may not always be explicit, but to help spot the variable we can ask questions like who, when and where?

Find the variable trail of breadcrumbs

Social science does not always use the language of variables, values and cases, but digging a little deeper will usually reveal that variables are there. Practising your thinking in terms of variables, values and cases helps you think more clearly about almost any social issue.

The more clearly and carefully a variable is defined, the better. Thinking about how to measure a variable is often a good way to do this. Since variables only manifest themselves through cases, it is important to be clear about just what those cases are.

USE LANGUAGE FOR CONTEXT CLUES

Quantitative research often explicitly discusses variables and describes how they have been defined, what cases they were based on, and the range of values they took, making the identification of variables easy.

Qualitative and historical research is often less explicit, and may use words like concept, theme, feature, characteristic or quality to refer to variables; or use a substantive name for an idea that is under discussion, such as 'class', 'gender' or 'violence'. This can make the variables harder to identify, but they will probably be there, under the surface!

You can use the variables' values and cases framework to spot variables when reading books or articles.

LOOK FOR THE DEFINITION

Variables should have some sort of clear definition. This is not about nit-picking or being a pedant, but rather understanding that conventional or 'obvious' definitions can be fuzzy or confusing.

For example, the concept of social class is widely used. But it could be defined in many ways, including

- subjective self-description
- type of occupation
- occupation of the main earner in a household
- educational qualifications
- area of residence

None of these definitions are right or wrong in themselves. We might think that even in using all of these definitions to approach the issue of class, there are aspects of the concept that we have missed. What matters is that you can tell what definition or meaning the author of any article or book is employing.

IDENTIFY THE WHO, WHEN AND WHERE

Variables will describe a definite collection of cases. Because we can only see variables by measuring cases, we can only describe or discuss the variables properly if we know which people, organizations or countries they refer to, and when and how the variable was measured.

A good question to ask of any evidence, especially numerical evidence, is 'where does it come from?' Reliable evidence always has a clear source.

A statement like 'In the 1970s, trade union membership grew in the UK, but declined in the USA' says nothing explicitly about variables, but it is based on a variable with values recording union membership, with the cases being workers in the 1970s in the UK and USA.

A statement like 'Attitudes towards homosexuality became more liberal in Western Europe towards the end of the twentieth century' might be based on survey evidence about attitudes, or the media representation of homosexuality, what public figures such as politicians or celebrities said about it, or other evidence like changes in legislation. However, we could still treat this in terms of a variable (attitudes) and how it changed for a group of cases (people in Europe at the end of the twentieth century).

DO IT YOURSELF

HOW TO SPOT THE VARIABLE

Find a journal article or a reading from your class and use it to fill in the exercise below. Some readings will be mostly or entirely 'theoretical', and not relevant, but others will use empirical evidence or describe the world.

List the variables the author discusses (you will probably identify several) and circle whether or not they define each variable explicitly.

Is it explicitly defined?

Variable 1 .... Yes / No / Partly

Variable 2 .... Yes / No / Partly

Variable 3 .... Yes / No / Partly

Variable 4 .... Yes / No / Partly

Need an example?

I've filled in the results at each step for an article from a recent issue of a sociology journal.

Variable 1 .... Types of work .... **Yes** / No / Partly

Variable 2 .... Commodification .... Yes / No / **Partly**

Variable 3 .... Precariousness .... **Yes** / No / Partly

Variable 4 .... Labour market flexibility .... Yes / **No** / Partly

Does the author discuss how these variables vary, or the values they take? Explain how (or how not).

Variable 1 ....

Variable 2 ....

Variable 3 ....

Variable 4 ....

Example article

Types of work: Detailed breakdown, e.g. part time, zero hours, self-employment

Commodification: No

Precariousness: Novn-standard / standard work

Labour market flexibility: High / Medium / Low

Does the author have a clear set of cases in mind?

Yes / No / Unclear

If so, what are the cases?

....

Example article

Yes; workers in six countries, recent labour legislation in these countries

What are the author's sources as evidence?

....

Source 1 ....

Source 2 ....

Source 3 ....

Example article

Case studies

Examination of employment regulation changes

Got it?

Q: How do you avoid fuzzy thinking and clearly identify the variable of a study?

Got it!

A: Be clear about the definitions of the variable and which cases the study is considering – you may have to dig beyond the explicit language!

There are two main kinds of variable

4 Section

Which variables measure quantities and categories?

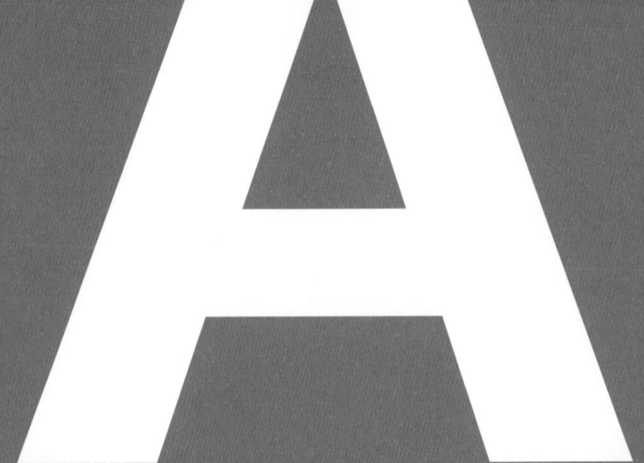

Continuous variables measure quantities and categorical variables measure categories.

Two kinds of variable

Because aspects of the social world vary in different ways, we have two kinds of variable to measure these different types of variation.

Continuous variables describe something that varies in a way that can only be described numerically, like a person's income. These variables always refer to the quantity of something. We can only describe how small or large it is, and the range of possible values is almost infinite.

Categorical variables involve a list of mutually exclusive categories or discrete values that can be classified and given different names. We can only describe these categories.

DESCRIBING QUANTITIES

If you look back at the variables you used to describe yourself in Section 2, you will see that some, like height, weight, age, income or hours spent studying last week, describe a quantity of something that can vary continuously. The values for these variables take a directly meaningful numerical value. Your age might be 19, weight 58 kilos, and you spent 23 hours last week studying. We call such variables continuous variables.

Continuous variables always describe the quantity of something. It is possible to have more or less.

SUMMARIZING AND MAKING COMPARISONS

Because we can use numbers to describe these quantities, we can use continuous variables to make all kinds of summaries or comparisons. I could compare the income of different individuals, or work out the average income for a group of people, or record the minimum and maximum incomes.

Continuous variables are sometimes called quantitative, interval or ratio variables.

DESCRIBING CATEGORIES

You will also see that some of the variables you used to describe yourself do not vary continuously in this way, but instead take the form of categories. You can only have been born in one place. You either are or are not a student. It is not possible to be more or less pregnant, or more or less dead, or half a member of something, in the way in which one can be shorter or taller. **When variation is about classifying things into different categories we have categorical variables.** The values for categorical variables take the form of lists of categories.

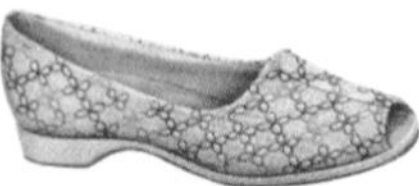

DESCRIBING INDIVIDUALS

Most of the variables we use to describe individuals are categorical. For example, the categorical variables in the Section 2 checkpoint were

Variable	Values
Union membership	Member Not a member
Views on homosexuals being free to live as they wish	Agree Disagree
Race identity	White Hispanic Black Asian

USING CATEGORIES TO FIND PROPORTIONS

Because categorical variables do not describe numerical quantities, there are fewer kinds of summaries we can make with them. We cannot take a group of people and calculate their average marital status in the way we could talk about their average income.

Instead we are usually interested in what proportion of people fit into each of the categories, or the distribution of cases across the values of the variable. I might summarize the marital status of a group of people by saying '50% are married or cohabiting, 30% are single and 20% are separated, divorced or widowed'.

ESTABLISHING CATEGORY CLASSIFICATION SYSTEMS

Classification systems must have two characteristics: the categories must be mutually exclusive, so that no observation can be put into more than one category; and they must be comprehensive, so every imaginable observation can be covered.

The UK Labour Force Survey variable on 'place of birth' includes not only every country in the world, but also the category 'at sea or in the air'. Around five in every million births take place there. Ensuring the categories of a variable are comprehensive explains why questionnaires usually contain the response 'other': it's a useful catch-all.

Categorical variables are sometimes called qualitative or *nominal* variables.

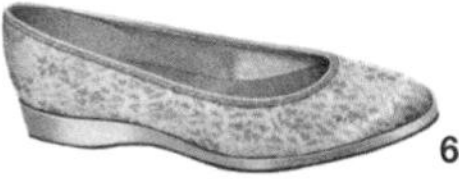

IDENTIFYING CONTINUOUS AND CATEGORICAL VARIABLES

Label each of the possible variables below as either 'continuous' or 'categorical'. Remember: are they describing a quantity or category?

1 Person's marital status ....

2 Person's age ....

3 Number of employees of a firm ....

4 Population of a country ....

5 Person's annual income ....

6 Belief in (a) God ....

7 Newspaper circulation ....

8 National identity ....

9 Whether person drinks alcohol ....

10 Unemployment rate for a country for successive months ....

11 Units of alcohol consumed last week ....

12 Frequency of attendance at church ....

CHECKPOINT

Answers

1 Categorical.
2 Continuous.
3 Continuous.
4 Continuous.
5 Continuous.
6 Categorical.
7 Continuous.
8 Categorical.
9 Categorical.
10 Continuous.
11 Continuous.
12 Continuous.

CONGRATULATIONS

Section 5

Examine categorical variables through tables, and continuous variables through scatterplots

How do I examine relationships between variables?

You use tables to look at relationships between categorical variables and scatterplots to look at relationships between continuous variables.

Relationships are the core of social science

Making comparisons and looking for relationships between variables are the essential core of all social science. We can use contingency tables, or 'crosstabs', to look at relationships between categorical variables by setting out the values of one variable by the values of a second variable, for the same group of cases. On the other hand, we can use scatterplots to examine relationships between continuous variables by showing the combination of values for two variables that each case takes.

THE SUM IS GREATER THAN THE PARTS

While a lone variable can tell us about the world, the essence of most social science is looking at how variables relate to each other. Most people accept homosexuality today, but the picture only a few decades ago was different. There is a relationship between time and views on homosexuality. I might also find a relationship to variables like age, religious belief, country and level of education.

The World Health Organization recently reported that, globally, just over 4 million children died in 2016 before reaching their first birthday. It is a shocking figure – even one infant death is a tragedy. But looking at it on its own overlooks progress achieved in combatting infant mortality. The global rate has halved in the last two decades. The current rate for the entire world is now only a little above that of Europe 50 years ago. Associating one variable (infant mortality) with other variables (place, time) tells us much more.

IDENTIFYING ASSOCIATIONS

There are two mains ways of looking at associations between variables

1 contingency tables ('crosstabs') for categorical variables

2 scatterplots for continuous variables

UNDERSTANDING CROSSTABS

Contingency tables show the proportion of cases taking each value for one variable, contingent upon or conditional upon, the values of a second variable. This sounds much more complicated than it actually is. Contingency tables are sometimes referred to as 'cross-tabulations', or 'crosstabs' for short. Table 1 (based on the European Social Survey data for 2016) looks at attitudes towards homosexuality contingent upon religious belonging.

(DIS)AGREEMENT WITH THE STATEMENT 'GAYS AND LESBIANS SHOULD BE FREE TO LIVE AS THEY WISH' BY RELIGIOUS BELIEF

(Column %)	No religion	Protestant	Roman Catholic	Islamic	Eastern Orthodox	All
(Strongly) Agree	72	83	76	41	17	67
Neither agree nor disagree	9	9.4	13	16	16	11
(Strongly) Disagree	19	7	12	44	67	22
Total	100	100	100	100	100	100
N	16,999	4070	13,500	1535	4858	40,962

How to get your head around what the table says

You can think of a contingency table as a postbox with a series of pigeonholes. Each pigeonhole corresponds to a combination of values for each of the variables represented in the table. So the first number in the table (72) corresponds to respondents who were

- not religious
- agreed with the statement

The table cell to its right (83) corresponds to respondents who were

- Protestant
- Agreed with statement

Two cells below this is the cell (7) corresponding to those who were

- Protestant
- disagreed with the statement

Arranged like this, the table shows the proportion of respondents who agreed or disagreed with the statement, within each religious group. Numbers in the table are percentages based on the total number of people in each religious group, shown at the bottom of each column of the table. We can see at a glance that, while non-believers, Protestants and Catholics tended to have liberal views, Muslims were more divided, and Eastern Orthodox believers were strongly against homosexuality. Using percentages means we do not have to worry that there were ten times as many people who described themselves as having no religion as there were Muslim respondents.

UNDERSTANDING SCATTERPLOTS

Just as a table has a cell or pigeonhole for each combination of values, in a scatterplot **each combination of values is represented by a single point or coordinate on a graph**. The graph has two axes. The horizontal or X-axis gives the range of values for one of the variables (in the figure below, average life expectancy in years). We plot the other variable (average life satisfaction) on the vertical or Y-axis. Each coordinate in the scatterplot represents the combination of the values for the two variables for a country, and some of them have been labelled. This figure looks at the life expectancy versus life satisfaction in different countries.

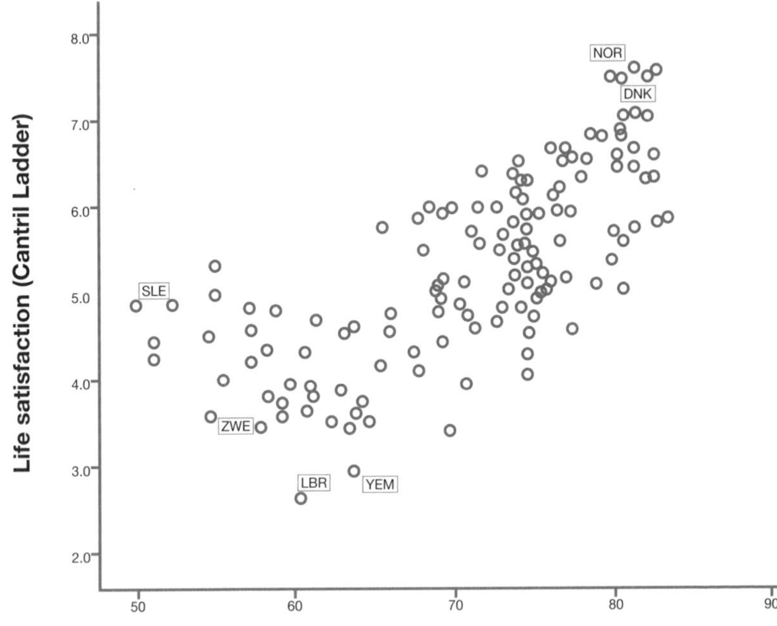
Life satisfaction (Cantril Ladder)
8.0
7.0
6.0
5.0
4.0
3.0
2.0
NOR
DNK
SLE
ZWE
LBR
YEM
50
60
70
80
90
Life Expectancy (years)

How to get your head around what the scatterplot says

Looking at specific coordinates, average life expectancy in Sierra Leone (SLE) was about 50 years, and life satisfaction about 5/10. Average life expectancy was above 80 in Norway (NOR) and Denmark (DNK) and satisfaction above 7/10. We can see from the pattern of the coordinates that life satisfaction and life expectancy tend to go together, but also that the fit is not a perfect one. People in Sierra Leone have a shorter life expectancy on average than people in Liberia (LIB) or Yemen (YEM), but tend to be more satisfied with their lives.

Got it?

Q: What types of relationships do contingency tables and scatterplots show?

Got it!

A: Contingency tables show the relationship between two categorical variables. Scatterplots show the association between two continuous variables.

CONGRATULATIONS!

My confidence in reading contingency tables and scatterplots is now

/ 10!

section

One variable can be determined by one or more other variables

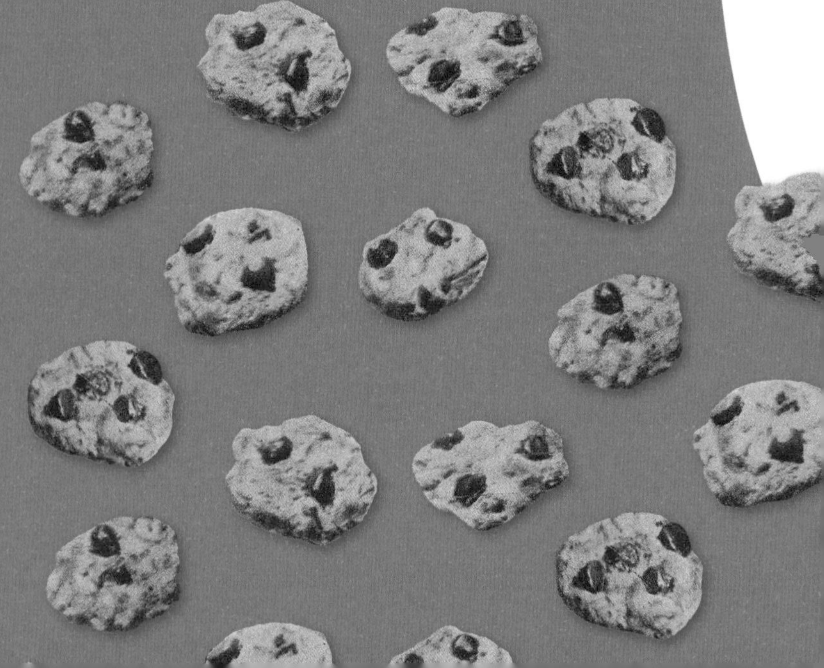

What are independent and dependent variables?

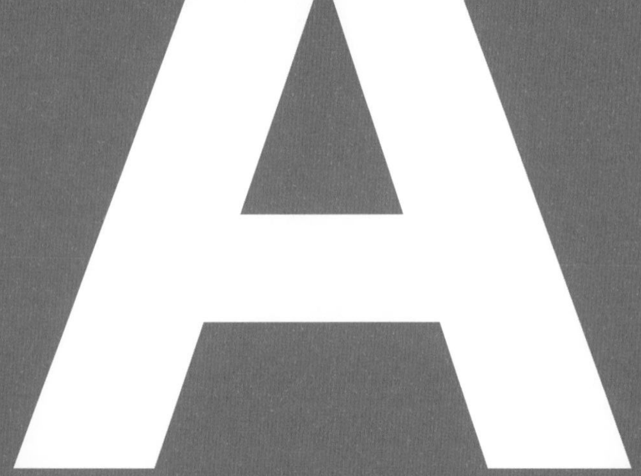

Independent variables are ones we think may determine the value of another variable. Dependent variables are ones whose values we think may be influenced by others.

Relationships between variables

Often we want to know if a relationship between two variables is one of cause and effect. Strong evidence about causation is often hard to get, except when we can run experiments where the value of one variable is manipulated and all the others are held constant. However, it is often useful to think in terms of independent and dependent variables where we suspect that one variable influences another.

THE CHALLENGE OF MANIPULATING VARIABLES IN SOCIAL SCIENCE

Natural scientists are often able to run experiments where they hold constant the values of all variables except one, and then examine whether it affects another variable. Clinical trials work in this way. Patients are randomly allocated to a treatment or a placebo and the results compared. Any difference in outcomes must have been caused by the treatment.

Social scientists usually cannot manipulate the values of variables in the same way. This would be impossible or unethical. For example, we could not force groups of randomly chosen children to be brought up in poverty in order to study its effects! However, it is still useful to think about how one variable might influence or be influenced by others.

THE CONNECTION BETWEEN DEPENDENT AND INDEPENDENT VARIABLES

The dependent variable is the one we are interested in and that we want to explain or account for. The independent variable(s) are the variables we use to look for associations with the dependent variable that might explain some or all of its variation.

Thus if we were interested in how attitudes to homosexuality had changed, we might be interested in what variables were associated with differences in attitudes. Section 5 demonstrated that religion is one possible influence, but there may be many others, like age, gender, class, political views, and so on. By looking at other characteristics of people with different views on homosexuality, we can begin to build a picture of how these views came to change.

HOW TO DECIDE IF A VARIABLE IS INDEPENDENT OR DEPENDENT

Whether we think of a variable as dependent or independent usually has little to do with the nature of the variable itself. Rather it depends on what we are interested in explaining.

However, there are some variables that are almost always treated as independent. Nothing determines a person's age other than the passage of time. Nor are there any known social determinants of sex at birth.

CHECKPOINT

Classifying dependent and independent variables

A researcher gathers data on the job satisfaction, occupation, sex, and relationship status of a sample of middle-aged people. Decide which could be the independent and dependent variables in the studies the researcher might make.

Dependent	Independents

All the other variables might plausibly influence job satisfaction. Job satisfaction is unlikely to influence occupation. The occupation or relationship status a person ends up in after education cannot influence what qualifications they obtained. However, sex still influences the level and subject of qualifications young people study.

Dependent	Independents
Job satisfaction	Occupation, highest educational qualification, sex, relationship status
Occupation	Highest educational qualification, sex relationship status
Highest educational qualification	Sex

Answers

section 7

Just because two variables are correlated does not mean one causes the other

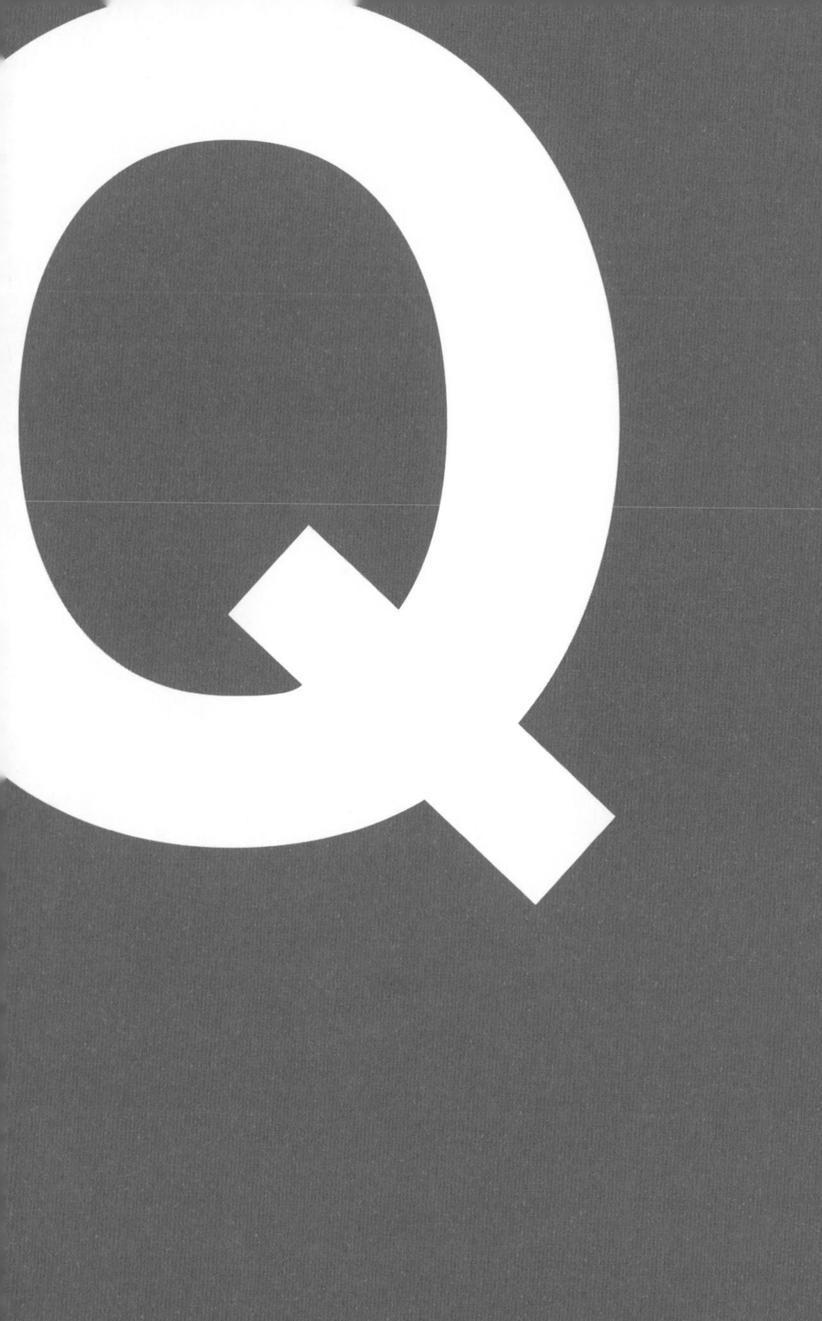

Why does correlation not automatically mean causation?

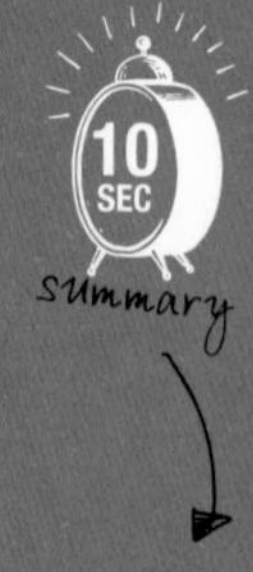

Correlated variables may also be impacted by other hidden variables.

Correlation is not causation

Two variables are correlated if their values tend to move together in some way. While a relationship, correlation or association between two variables is necessary for there to be a relation of cause and effect between them, this is not sufficient evidence for a causal connection. It is possible for each of two variables to be determined by a third, hidden or 'lurking' variable that is the genuine underlying cause. Just because two variables are correlated does not allow us to conclude that one causes the other, or the values of one variable influence or determine the value of another variable.

LOOK OUT FOR THE HIDDEN VARIABLE

Data from many times and places often shows a substantial association between ice cream consumption and the incidence of crimes like theft, mugging or burglary. The two variables are highly correlated. As ice cream sales rise, so does the incidence of these crimes.

However, this association is not causal. Banning ice cream and reducing ice cream sales would probably have no impact on crime. The correlation is a 'spurious' one.

A third, hidden or 'lurker' variable is responsible – the weather.

WHY YOU NEED TO CONSIDER THE FULL PICTURE

In sunnier, warmer weather more people are out and about, increasing opportunities for theft in public spaces and for burglaries in vacant homes. Burglars and pickpockets dislike heavy rain or cold winds as much as everyone else and stay indoors. More ice cream is sold when the weather is fine than when it is poor.

Tyler Vigen runs an amusing website illustrating examples of spurious correlations, like cheese consumption and the risk of death by becoming tangled in bedsheets (http://tylervigen.com/spurious-correlations).

DON'T CRY 'CAUSATION!' WITHOUT DUE DILIGENCE

When the correlation between cigarette smoking and lung cancer was first demonstrated, discussion and debate focused on whether the link was also causal. Research looked for lurker variables. Perhaps genetics, personality or some other variable predisposed people to lung cancer and also to smoking. Had such variables been identified, reducing cigarette consumption might have had as little impact on lung cancer as banning ice cream would have on crime. However, no such variables were identified. This correlation was indeed evidence of cause and effect.

BEWARE THE LURKER VARIABLES

Virtually everywhere in the world, women have fewer or lower educational qualifications, on average, than men. There is a correlation between educational qualifications and intelligence, so there must be a correlation between sex and intelligence. Intelligence cannot determine sex; therefore sex influences intelligence, and men are cleverer, on average, than women.

Spot the flaws in this argument and suggest some lurker variables below.

ANSWER

Educational qualifications depend not only on intelligence but also on access to education. In the past it was much harder for women than men to get to college or university. Since access has become more equal, women often outnumber men in gaining qualifications.

A range of other variables affect gender, or norms about what it is legal, possible, respectable or desirable for men or women to do. These may have nothing to do with any similarities or differences in intelligence or ability by sex.

section 8

How you use variables will depend on the kind of project you undertake

How can I use variables in my research project?

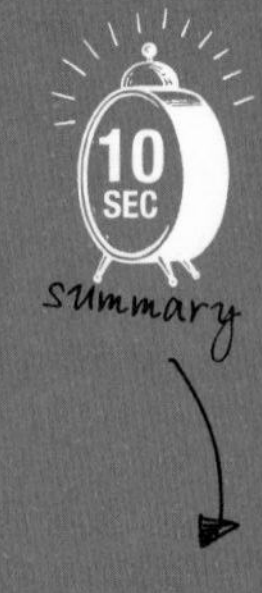

Variables are a useful way to organize your ideas for planning any research project.

Choose your variable, choose your research

Most research falls into two main types. Qualitative research is usually exploratory and can use a large number of variables, but cover only a small number of cases in depth. Quantitative research covers a much larger number of cases with more tightly defined variables. Having a clear idea about what types of comparisons you want to study and why will help you choose which type of research you should do.

USE YOUR VARIABLES AS A STARTING POINT

Thinking about variables is a useful place to start organizing a research project or dissertation. Consider what the relevant variables might be, where you would find information on them, and what new information, if any, you need to collect.

Do a literature review, noting what variables different authors use and how they define them. Does the same list of variables crop up repeatedly, or do different authors use different ideas or definitions?

Variables tend to be used in two different ways in empirical social research.

USING VARIABLES FOR IN-DEPTH EXPLORATION

Qualitative research often takes the form of in-depth exploration of a small number of cases through

- in-depth, open-ended or unstructured interviews
- observation
- documentary analysis
- diaries
- photographs, videos or other visual evidence
- biographical accounts

The aim is to explore people's accounts of their attitudes or behaviour, asking 'why' questions and focusing on narrative accounts in order to develop a fuller picture of the way people understand the world and act in it.

Because of their open-ended character, such methods can usually cover only a small number of cases. The aim is not to describe a representative sample (impossible with such small numbers), but to explore what the range of different people's experiences may be, and how they might relate together. Such exploration tends to produce empirical material that is difficult to squeeze into clearly defined variables that can describe every case in a limited range of values.

USING VARIABLES FOR COMPARING GROUPS OF PEOPLE

Quantitative research uses a much larger sample of cases, but with fixed response questions. Rather than directly asking respondents about their understanding, it uses variables and their associations to compare different groups of respondents.

Imagine a researcher wants to study why fewer young people go to university from some ethnic groups than others. Qualitative research might interview young people about their aspirations and attitudes, experience of education, family background and expectations for the future.

Quantitative research might compare young people from different ethnic groups in terms of educational qualifications, social attitudes, schooling, residence, family experience of higher education, and social class. Perhaps controlling for other social factors makes ethnicity less or more important. If the former, what appear to be differences due to ethnicity may have other social origins. If the latter, this might lead to a search for more directly discriminatory processes. Perhaps there are revealing differences across disciplines, or by university type.

CHECKPOINT

True/False

1 Qualitative research tends to use a large number of cases with fewer variables. True / False

2 Quantitative research uses many variables and a few cases. True / False

3 Making comparisons between groups is the focus of quantitative research. True / False

Answers

1: False (Qualitative research tends to use many variables and a few cases.)

2: False (Quantitative research uses a much larger number of cases, with many fewer variables.)

3: True (Comparisons guide us towards important relationships between variables.)

Work through this checklist to help ensure you have mastered all you need to know

- [ ] **Section 1:** Do you know why we need variables? If not, go back to page 9.
- [ ] **Section 2:** Do you understand what a variable is, and how you measure it? If not, go back to page 23.
- [ ] **Section 3:** Do you know how to use the variables' cases and values framework to identify variables in research? If not, go back to page 39.
- [ ] **Section 4:** Do you know what two kinds of values a variable can take? If not, go back to page 55.

HOW TO KNOW YOU ARE DONE

- [ ] **Section 5:** Do you know how to look at the relationship between two variables? If not, go back to page 71.

- [ ] **Section 6:** Do you know what independent and dependent variables are? If not, go back to page 89.

- [ ] **Section 7:** Do you understand the difference between correlation and causation? If not, go back to page 99.

- [ ] **Section 8:** Do you understand how qualitative and quantitative research uses variables in different ways? If not, go back to page 111.

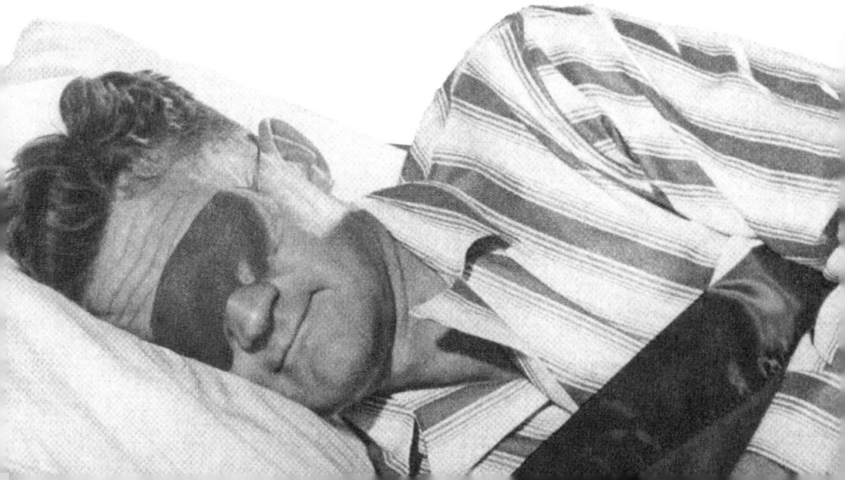

Glossary

Association Another term for correlation or relationship between two variables'.

Case An individual, organization or society that is a member of a sample or described by a variable.

Cause Producing a result, making something change or occur.

Categorical variable Variable whose values take the form of discrete, mutually exclusive categories.

Comprehensive The range of values for a variable covers every conceivable case.

Contingency table A table showing the distribution of values for one variable by the distribution values for a second variable. Also called a cross-tabulation or 'crosstab'.

Continuous variable Variable whose values take a directly meaningful number.

Correlation The degree to which the values of one variable vary with the values of a second variable.

'Crosstab' See contingency table.

Data Evidence in a numerical format, including the values of variables for a number of cases.

Dependent variable A variable whose values we try to account for using one or more independent variables.

Independent A variable that is thought to have some association with a dependent variable.

Interval variable See continuous variable.

Law A relationship between two variables that is thought to be universal and to describe some property of the world (e.g. gravity).

Lurker variable A variable whose association with each of two other variables causes these two variables to be correlated.

Mutually exclusive No case can take more than one value for the same variable.

Nominal variable See categorical variable.

Qualitative methods Methods that study a small number of cases in great depth.

Quantitative methods Methods that study a large number of cases, usually using a small number of variables.

Ratio variable See continuous variable.

Relationship Some link between two variables, such that the values of one variable tends to move in a consistent way with that of another variable. See also correlation; association.

Response variable See dependent variable.

Scatterplot A graph plotting the values of two continuous variables.

Spurious correlation A correlation that does not describe a relationship of cause and effect.

Value The result of the measurement of a variable for a case.

Variable A characteristic or feature of a group of cases that varies across these cases.

X-axis The horizontal axis of a scatterplot plotting the values of a variable.

Y-axis The vertical axis of a scatterplot plotting the values of a variable.